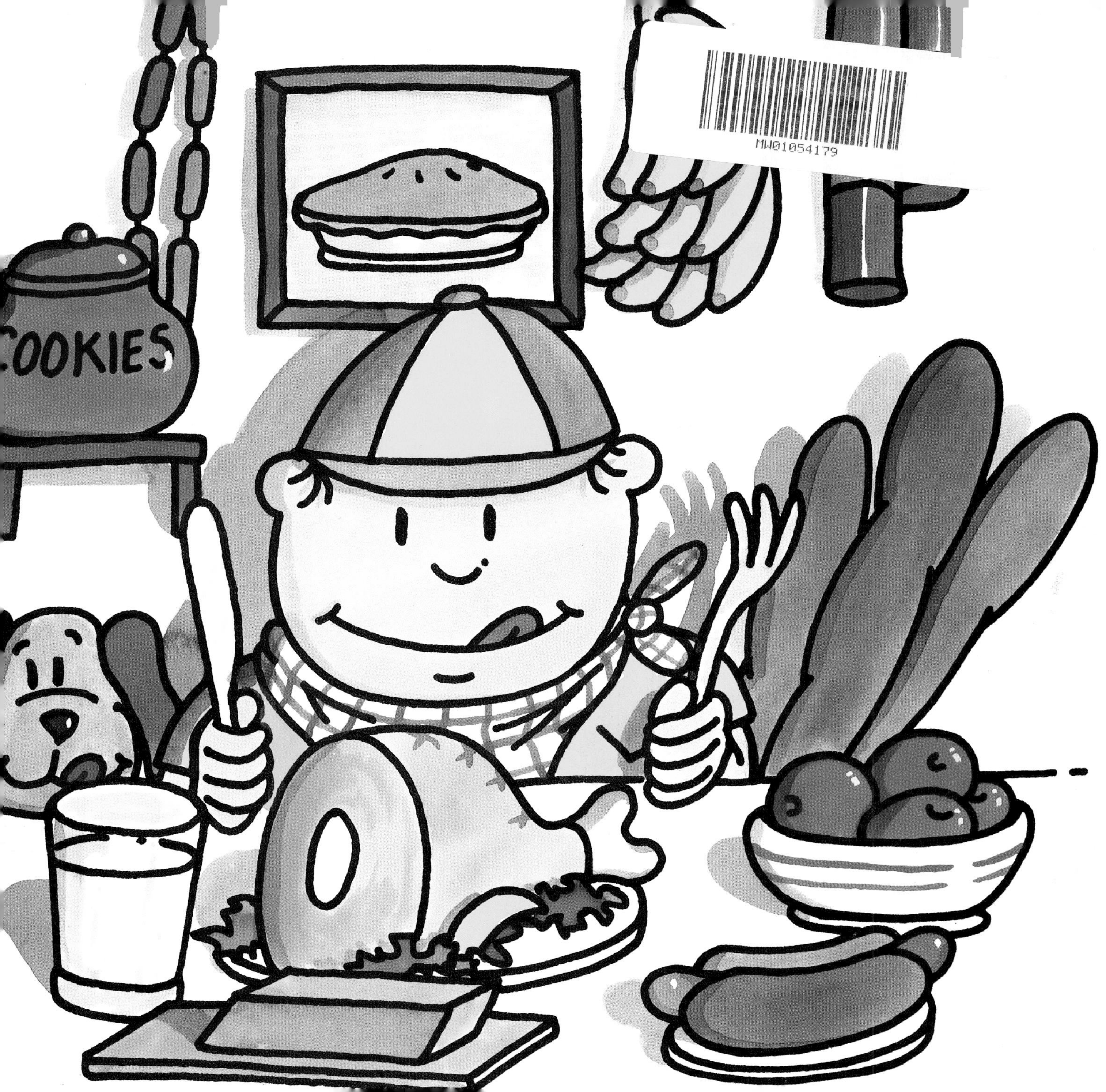

MW01054179

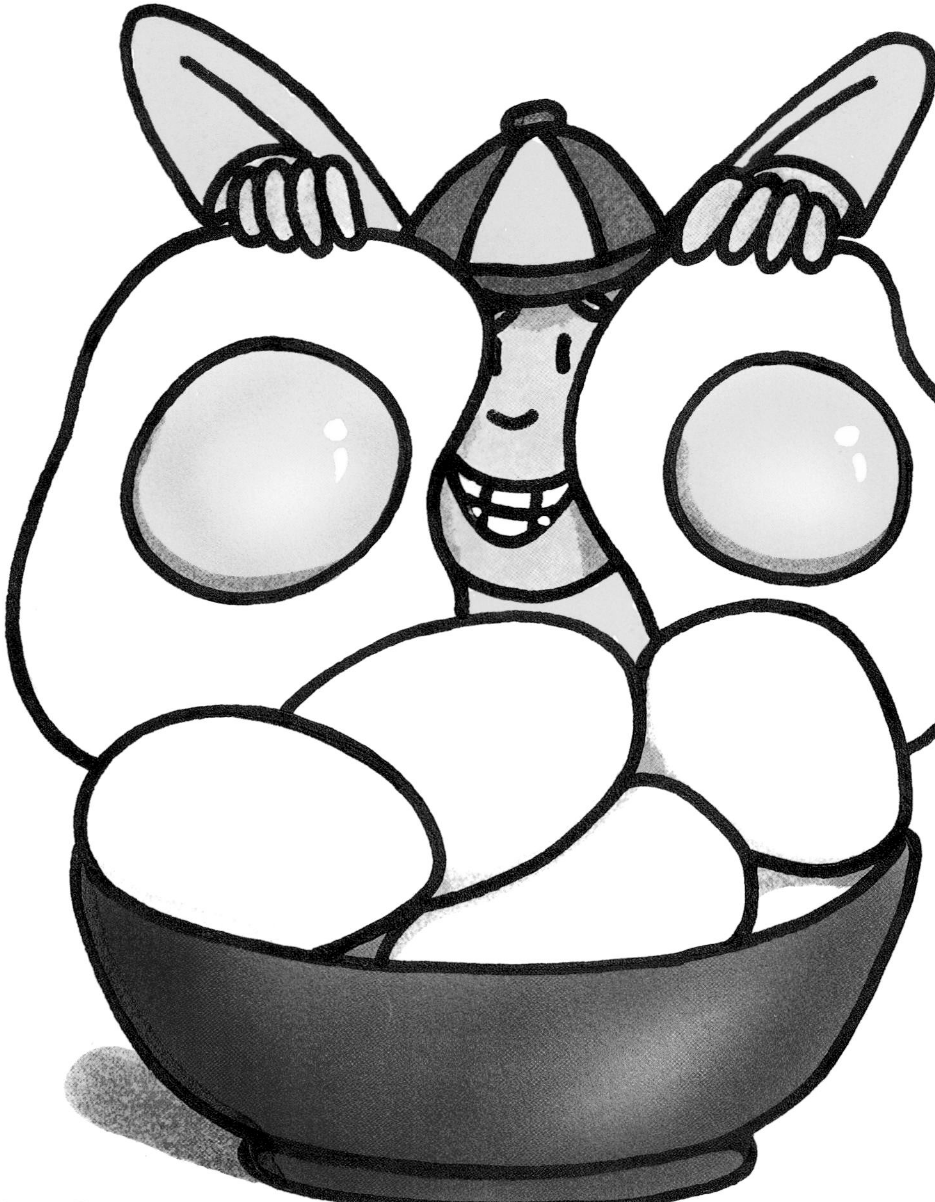

Eggs

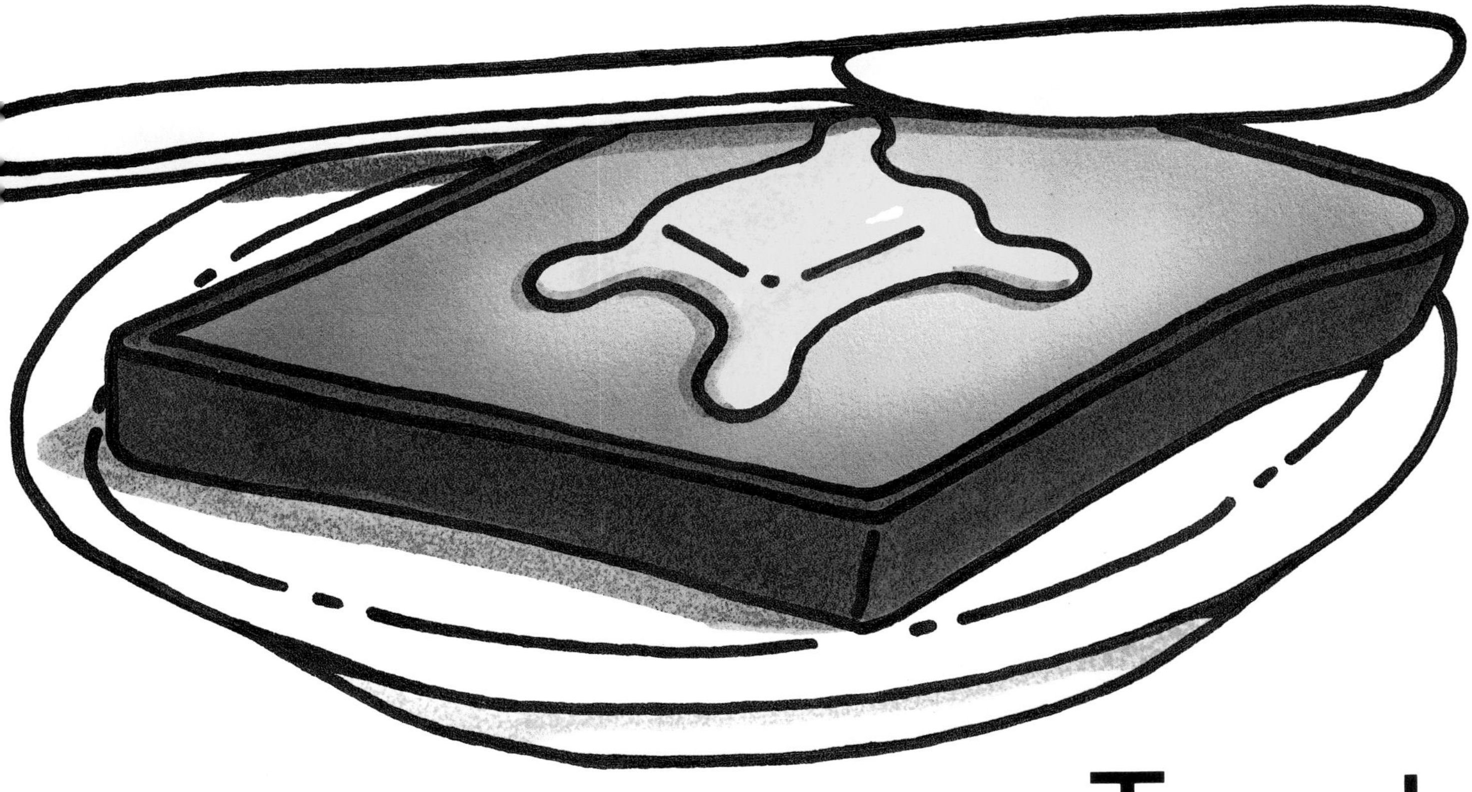

Toast

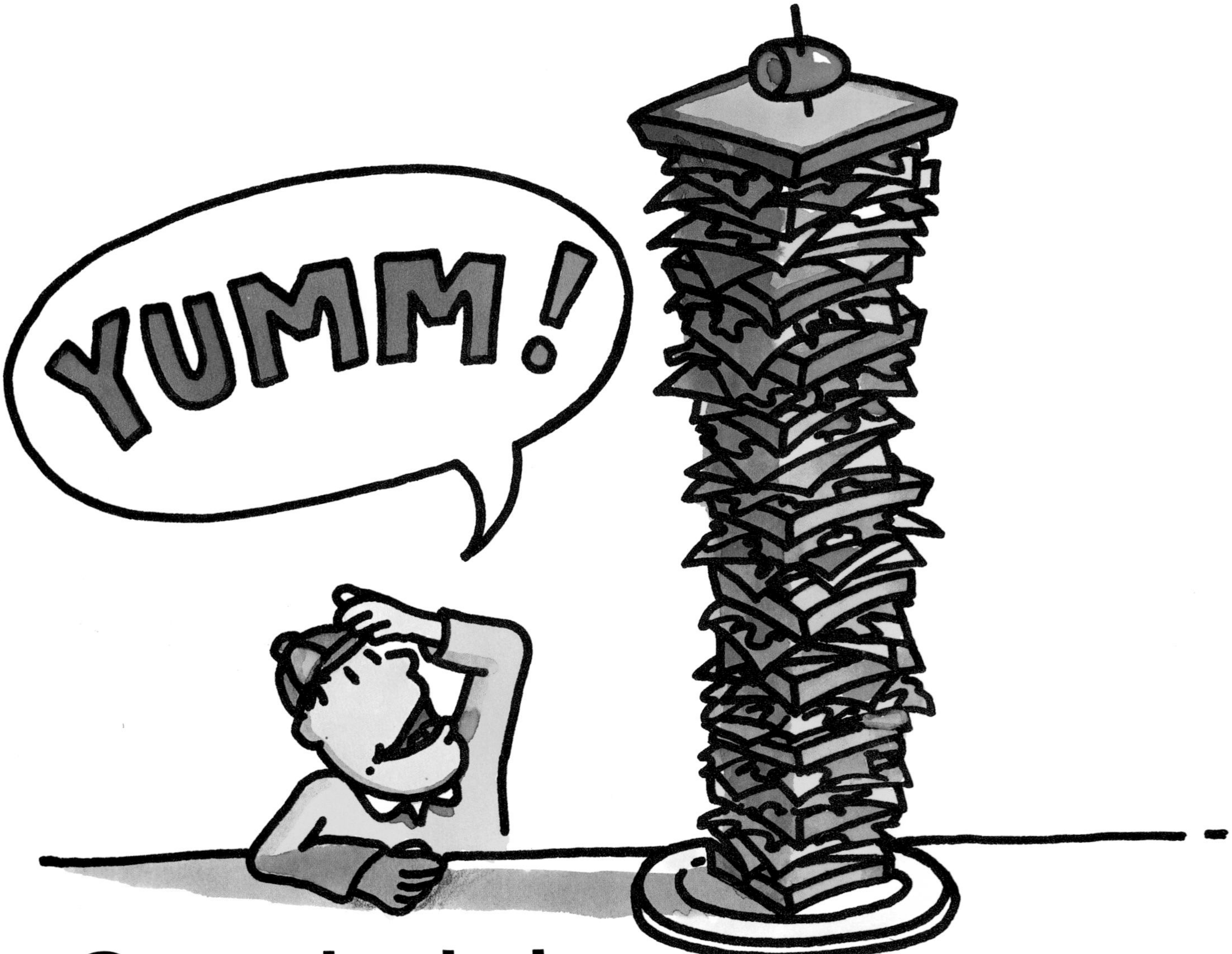

Sandwich

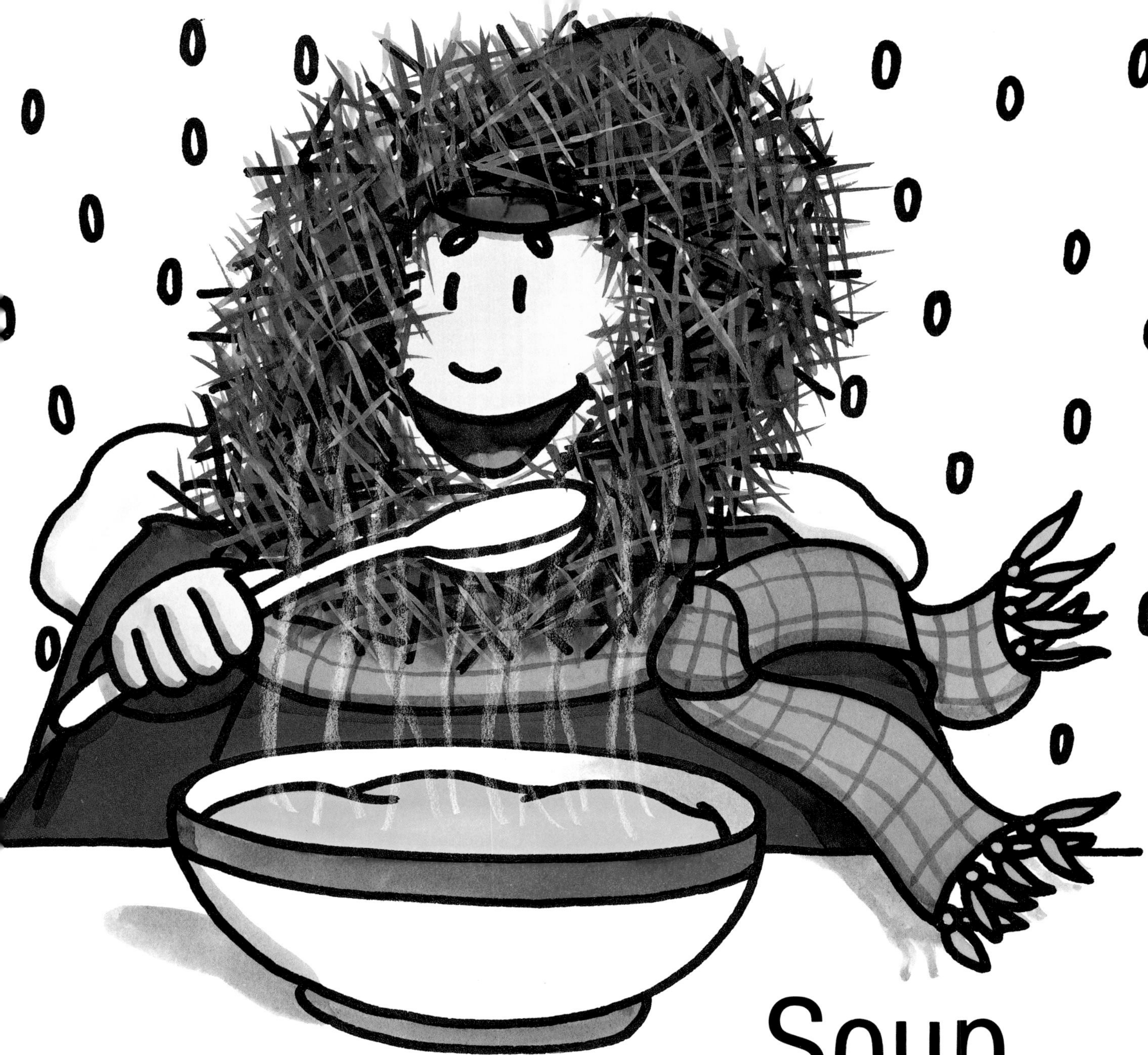

Soup

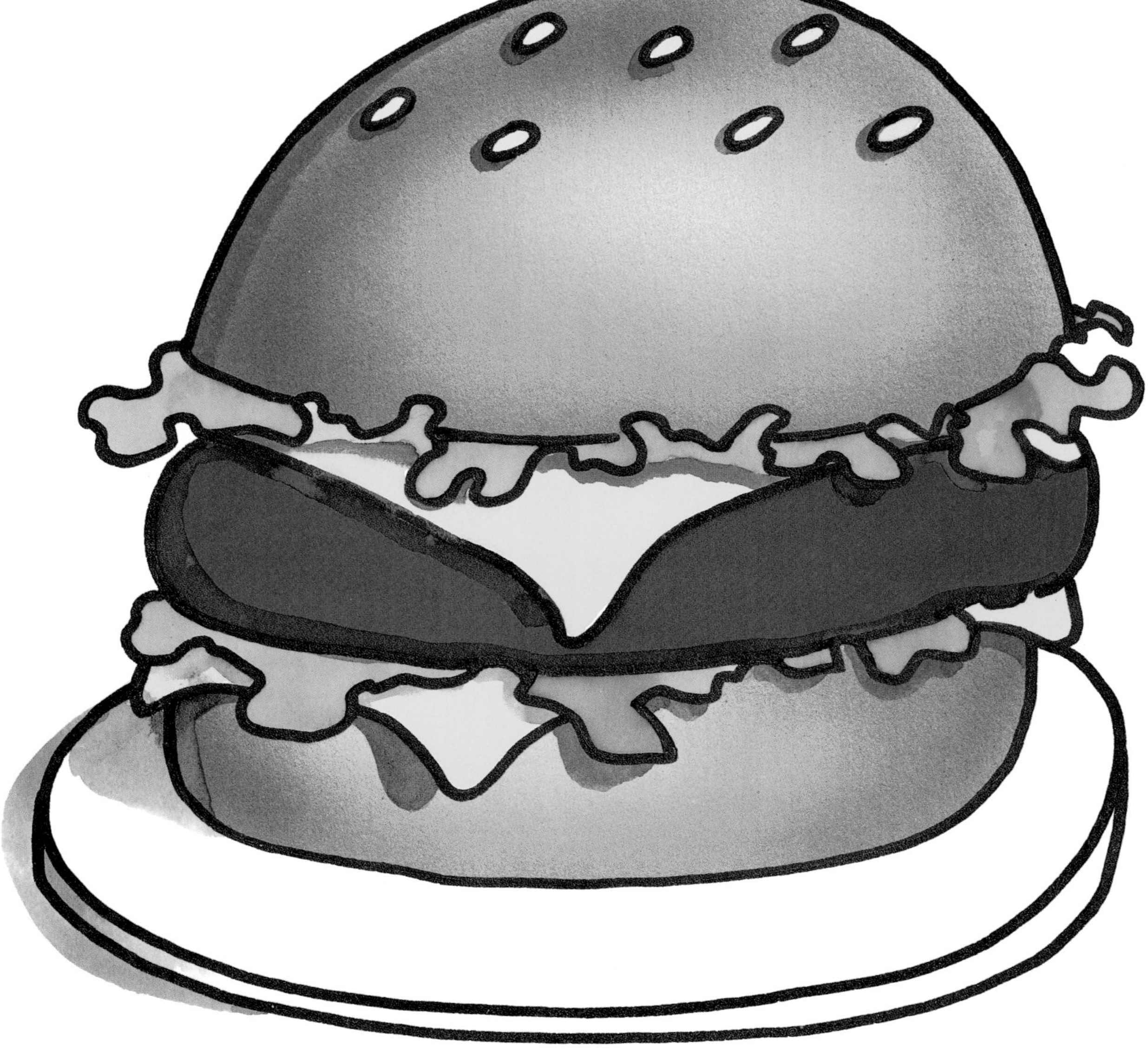

Hamburger

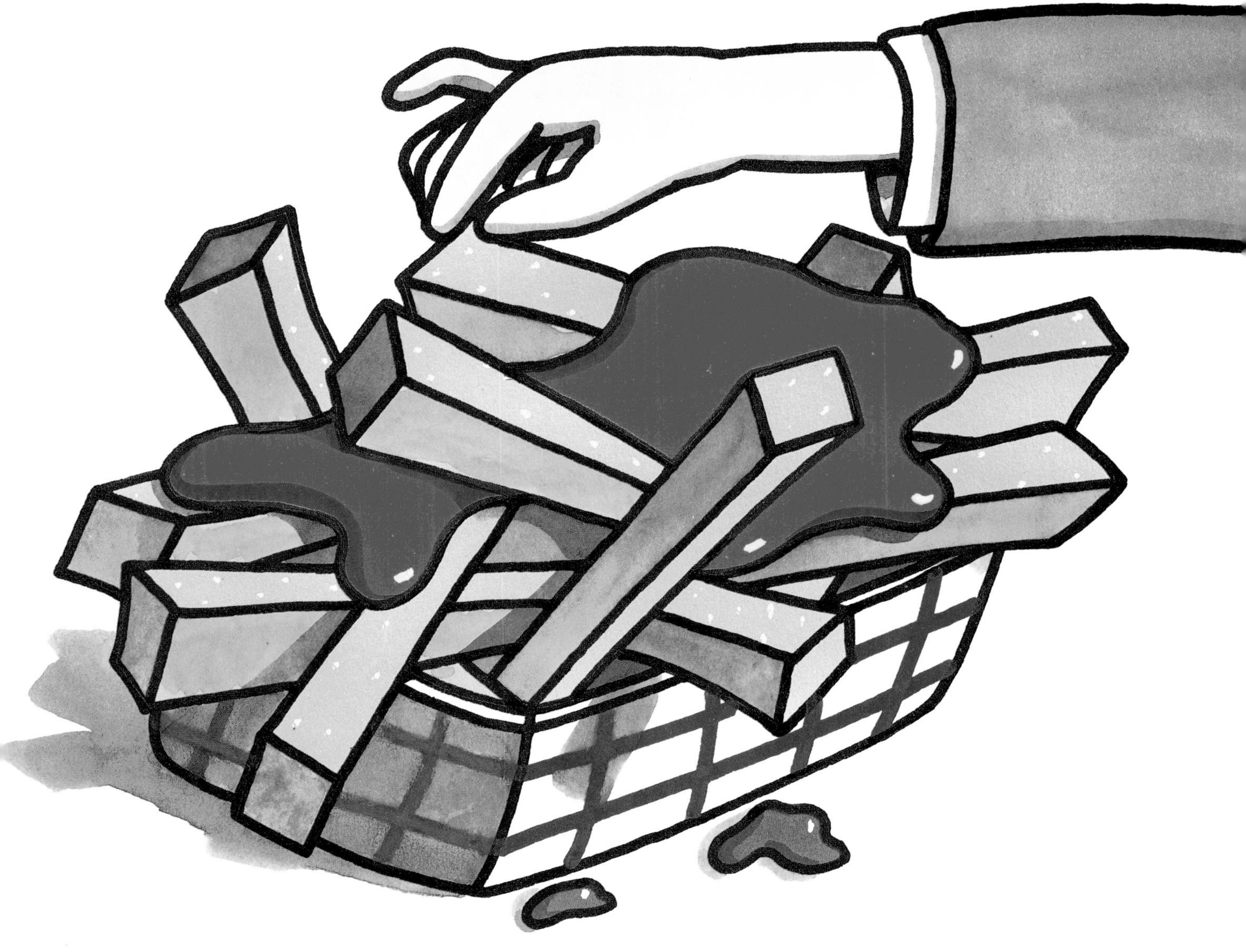

French Fries

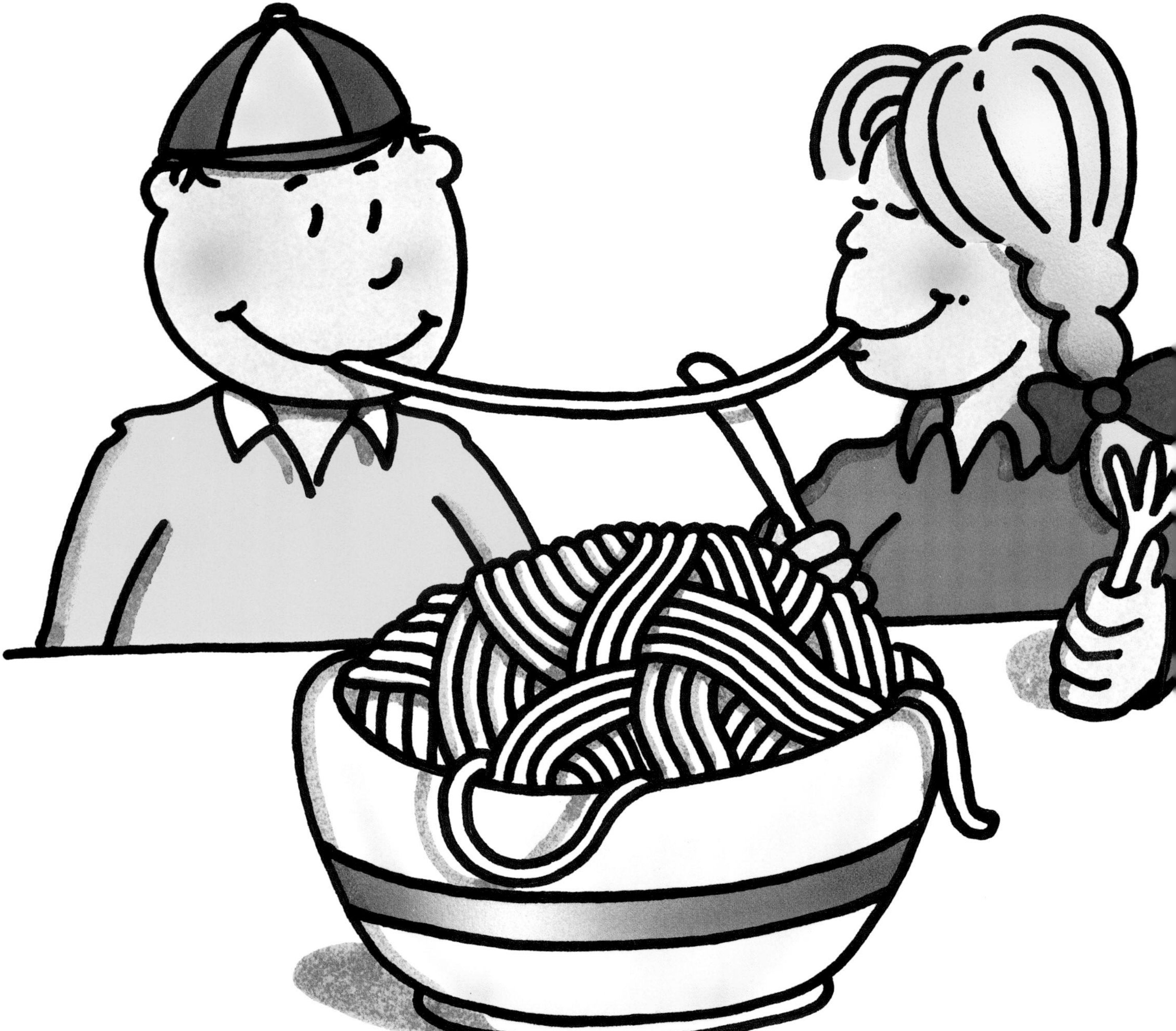

Spaghetti

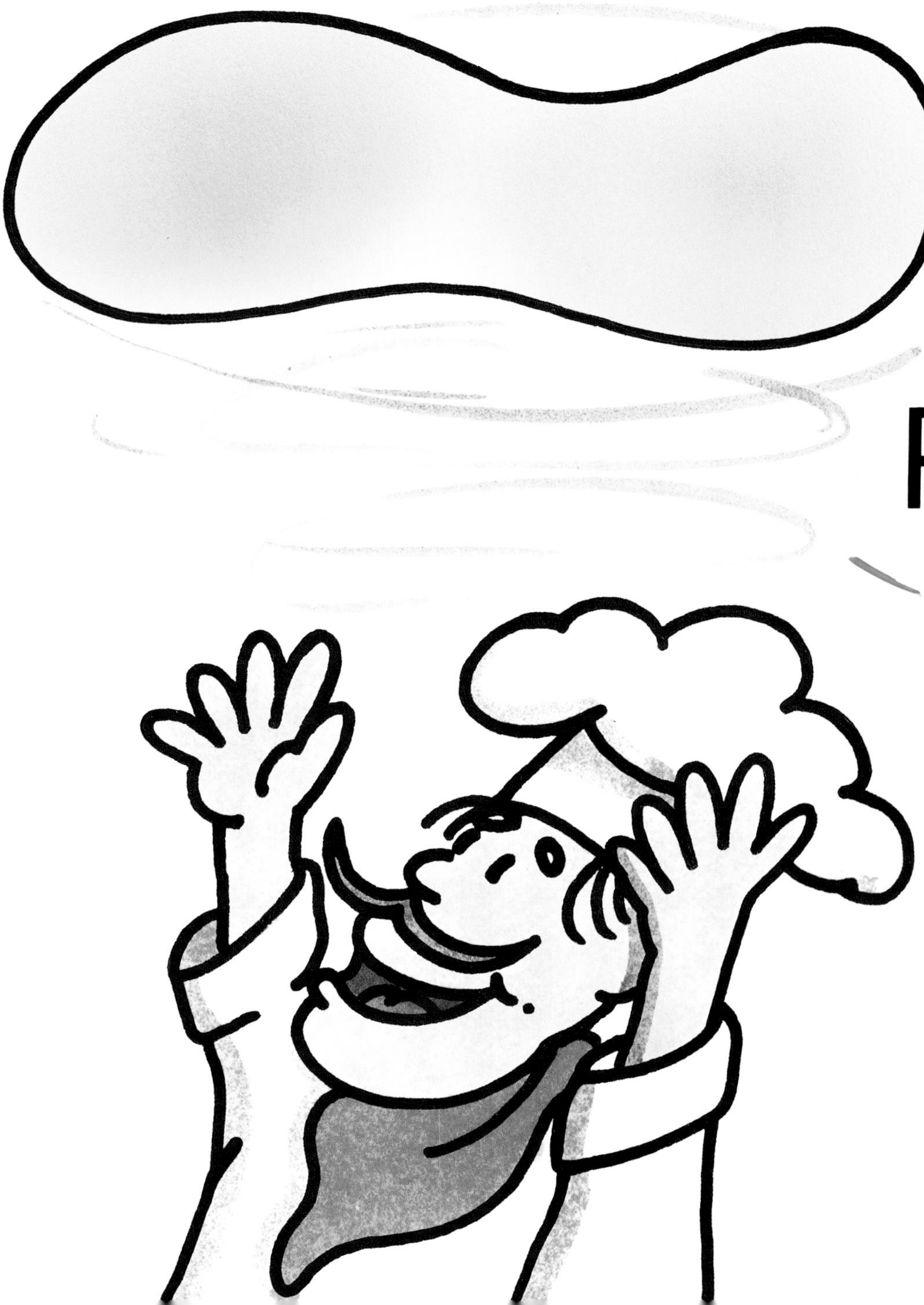

Pizza

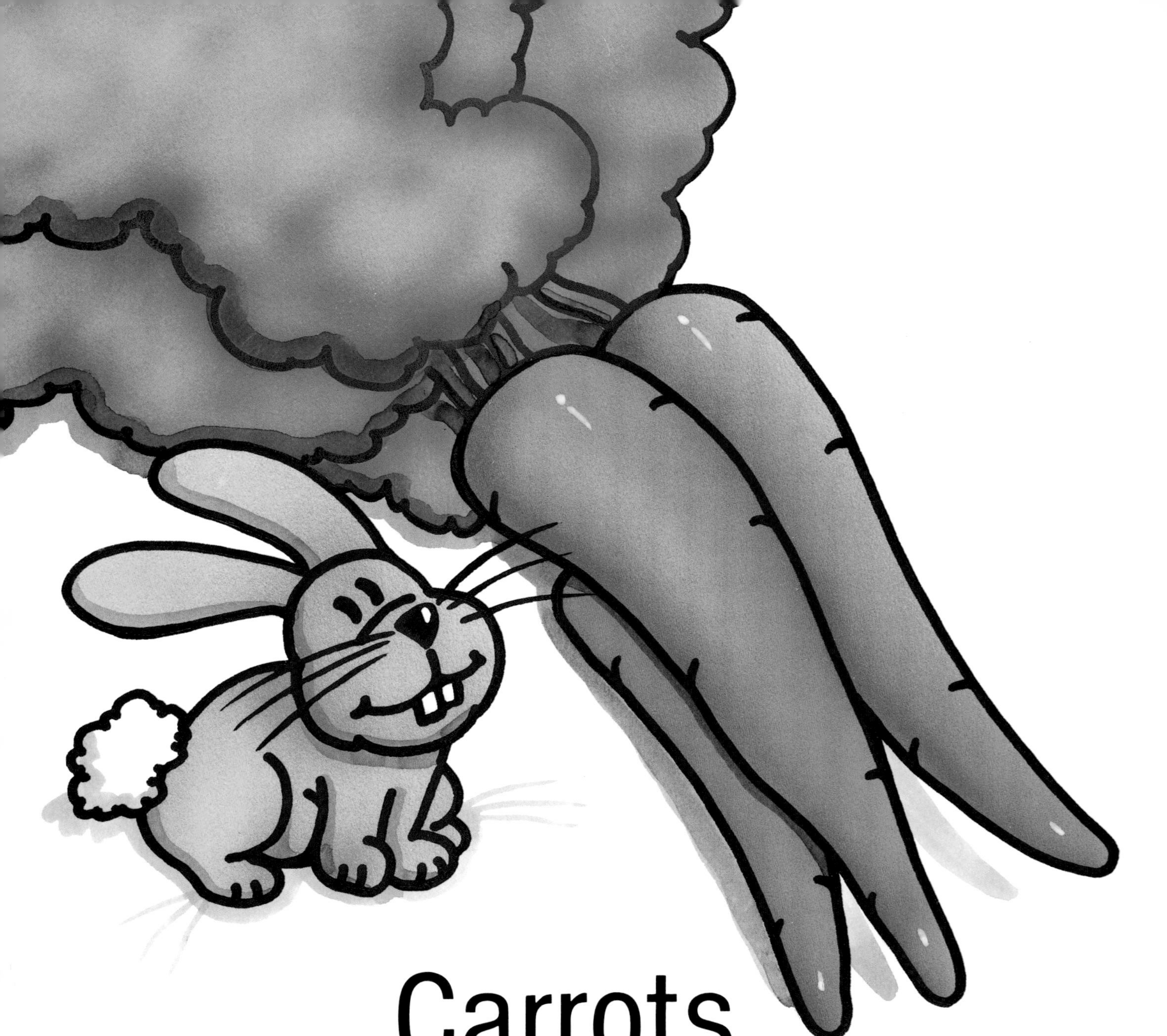

Carrots

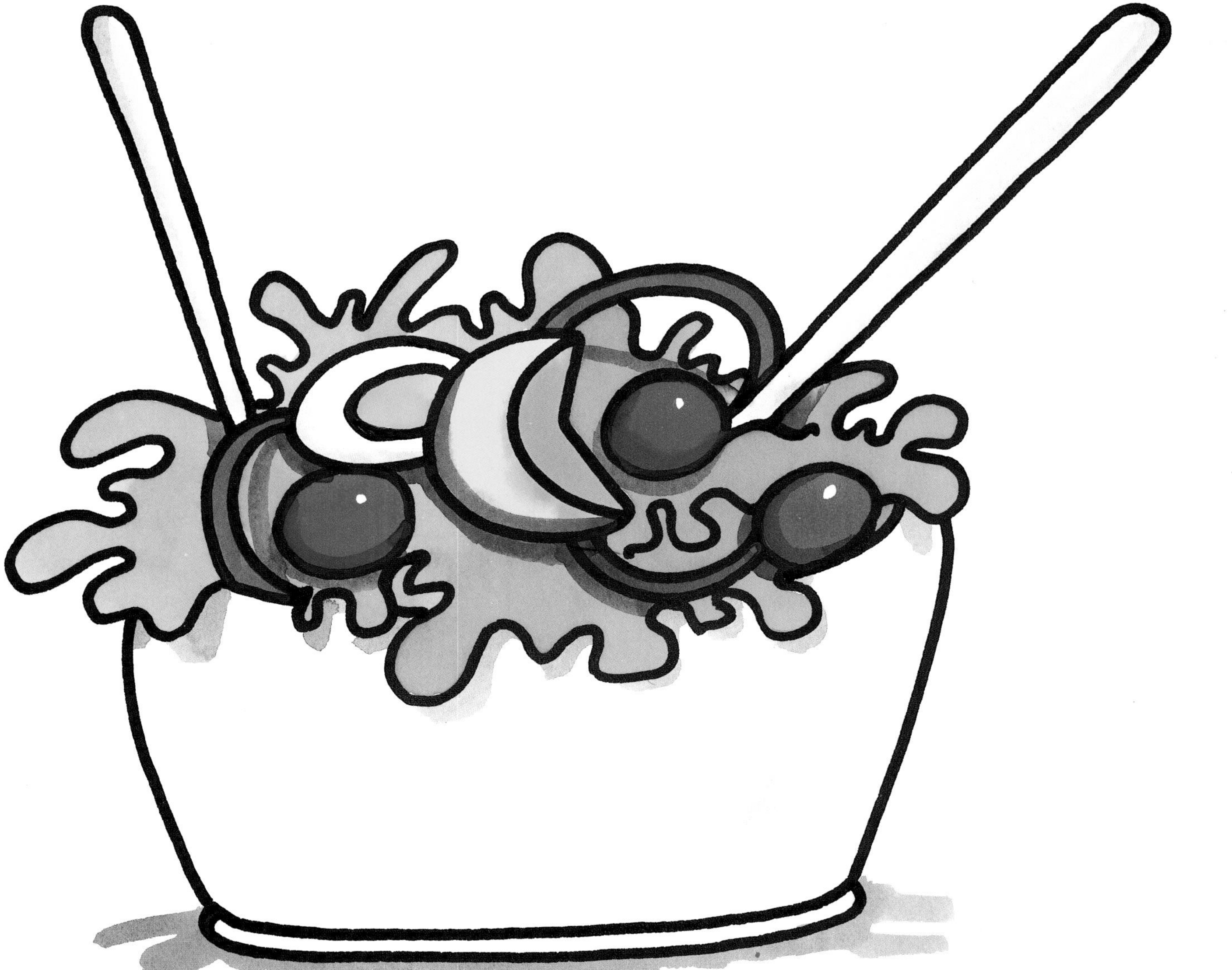

Salad

Apple

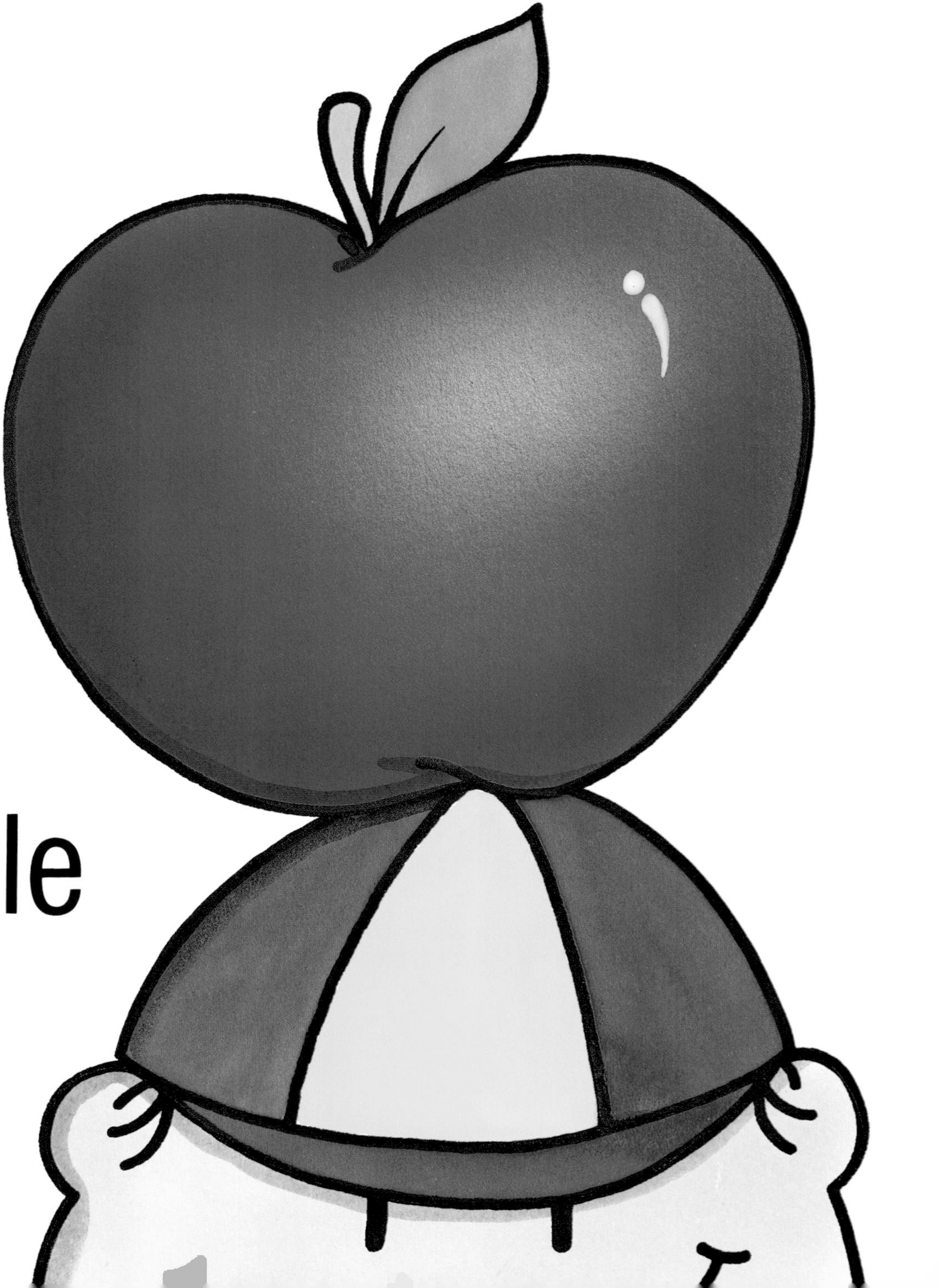

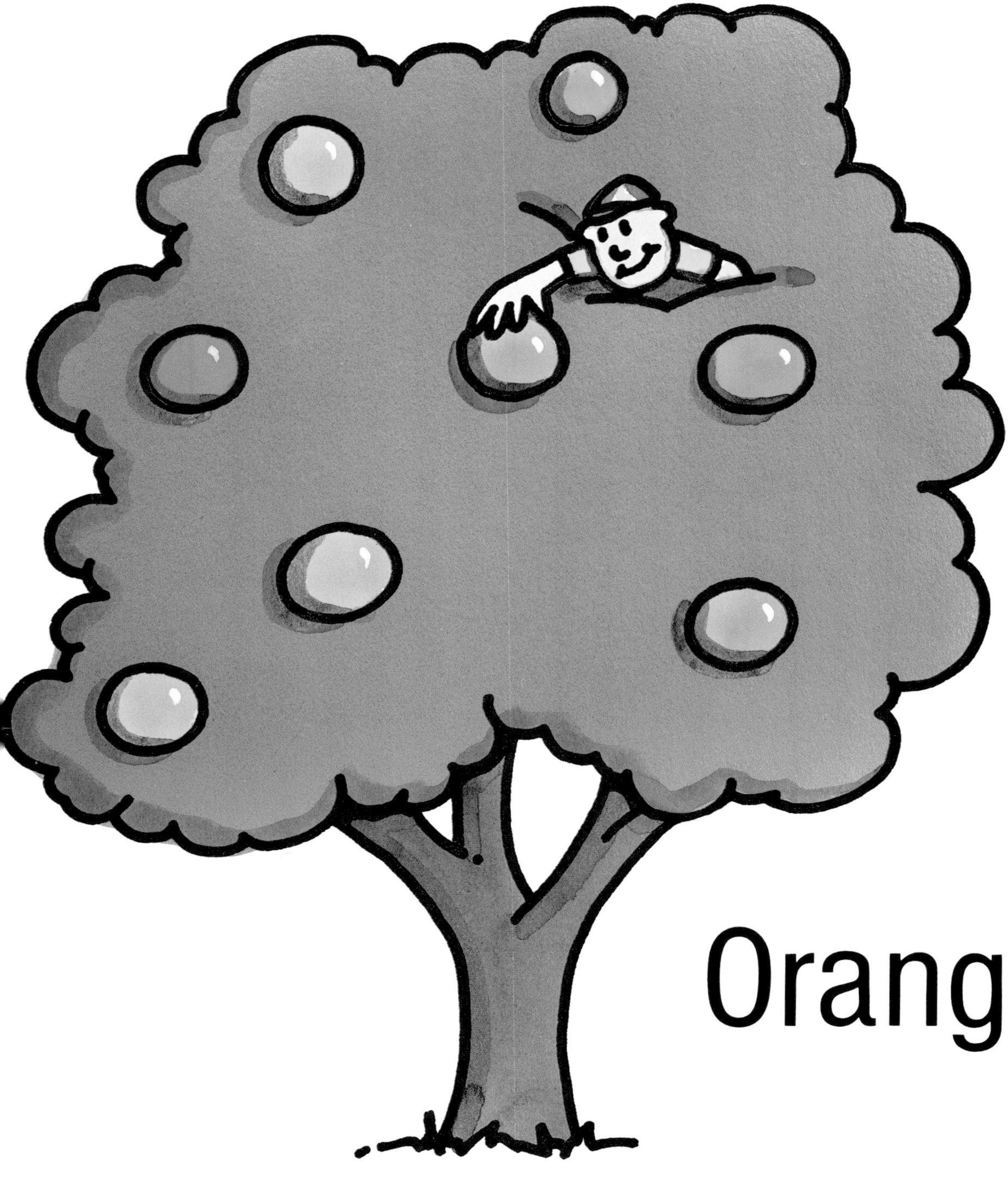

Oranges

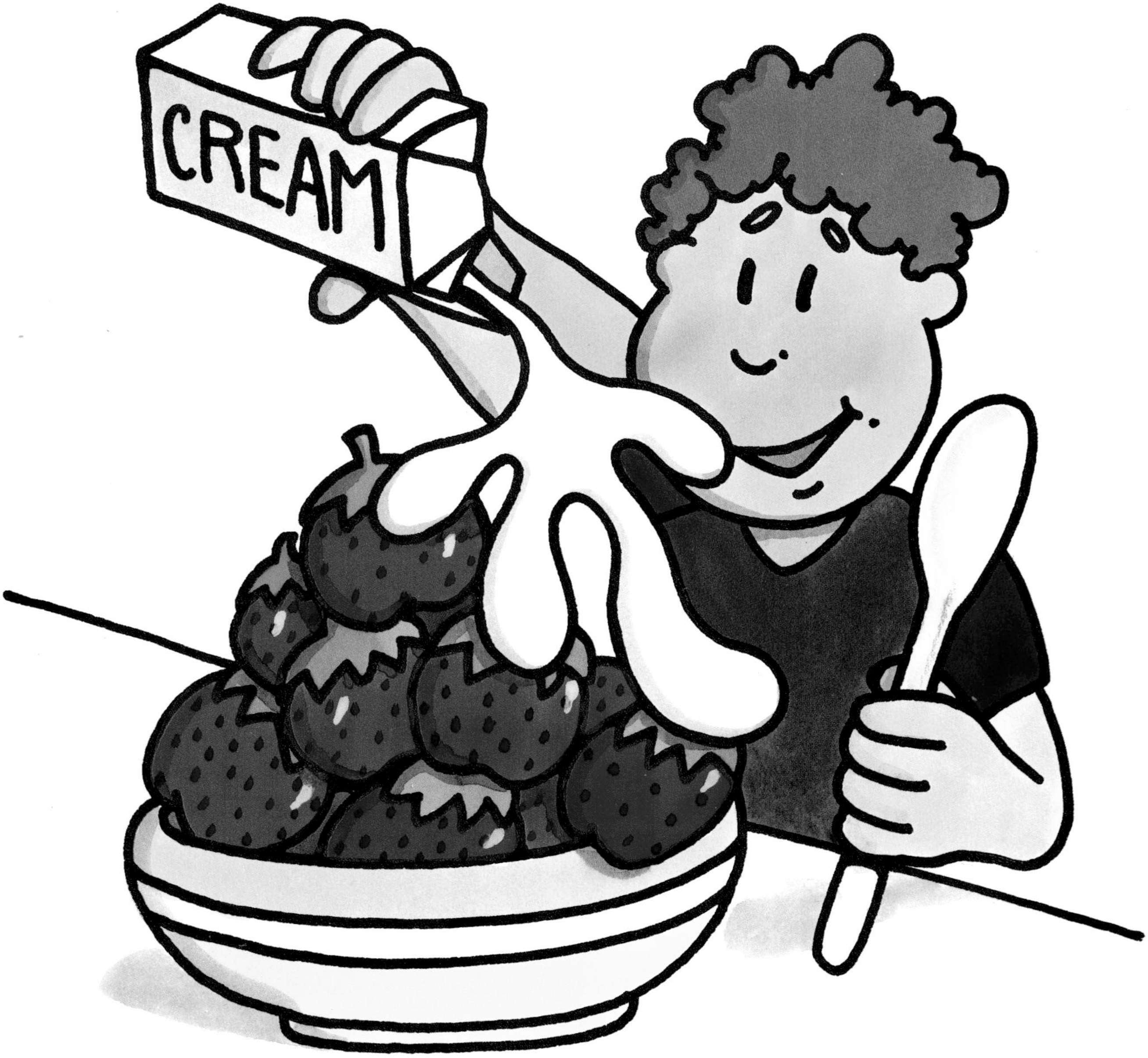

Strawberries

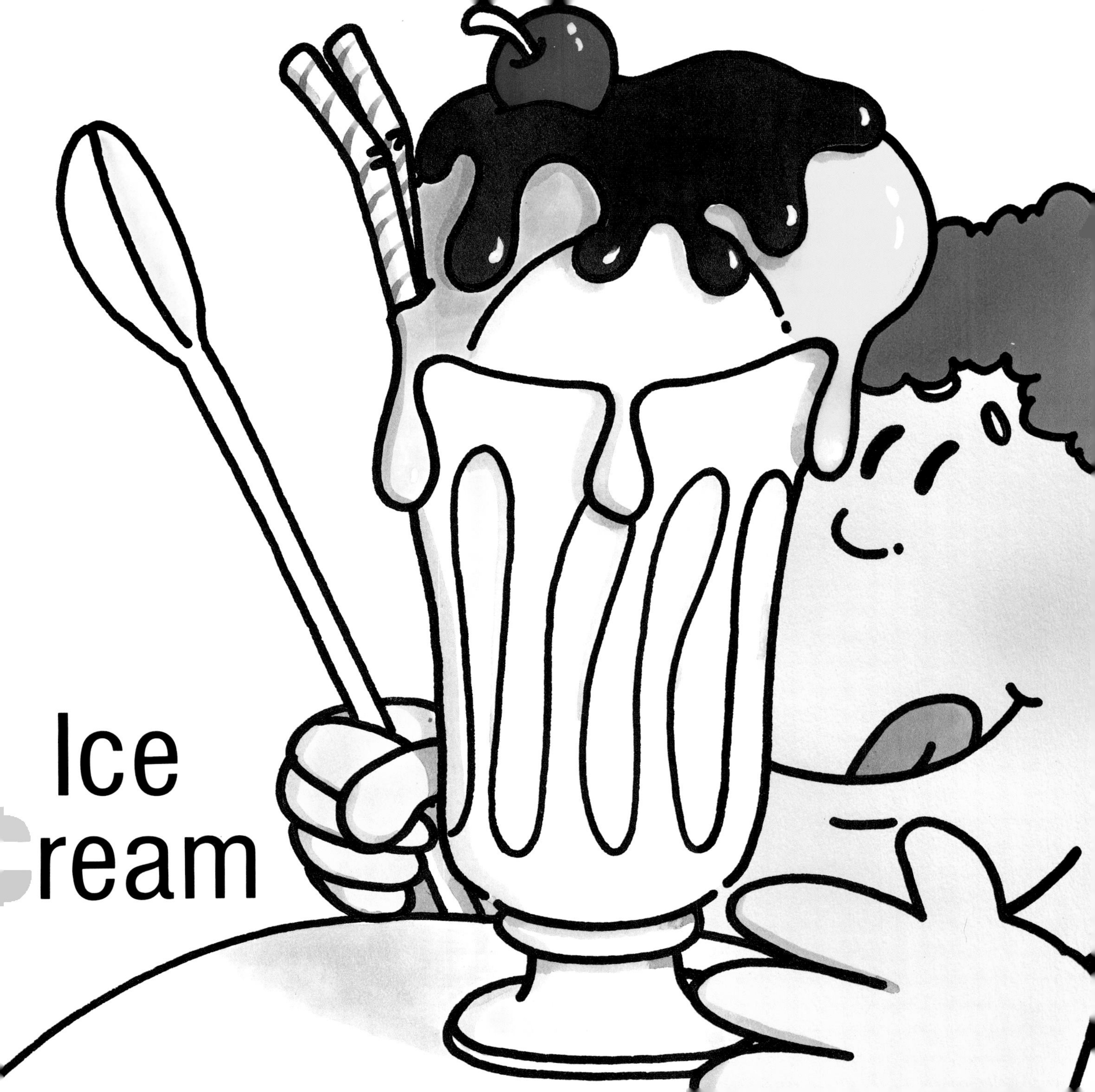
Ice
Cream

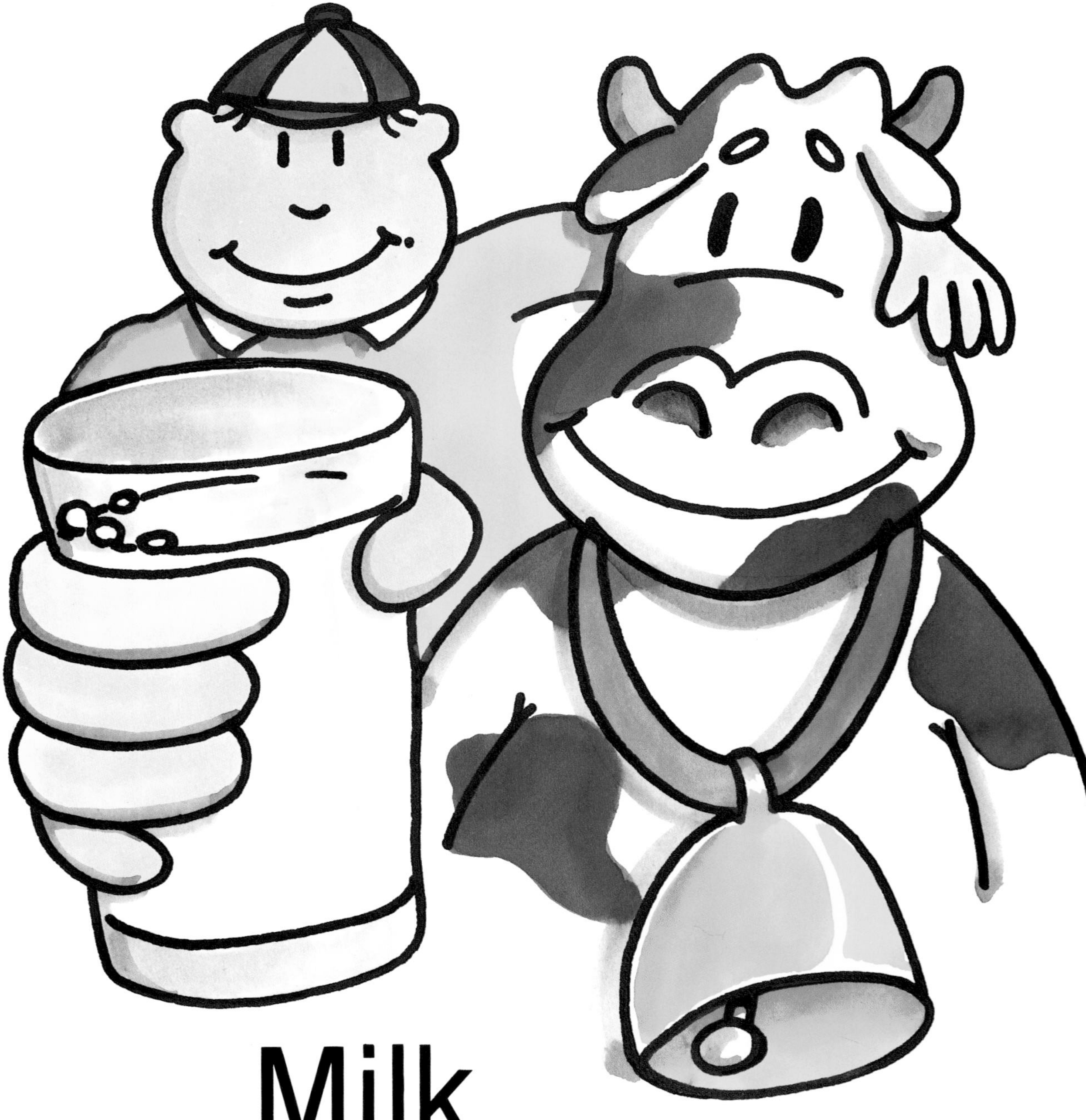

Milk

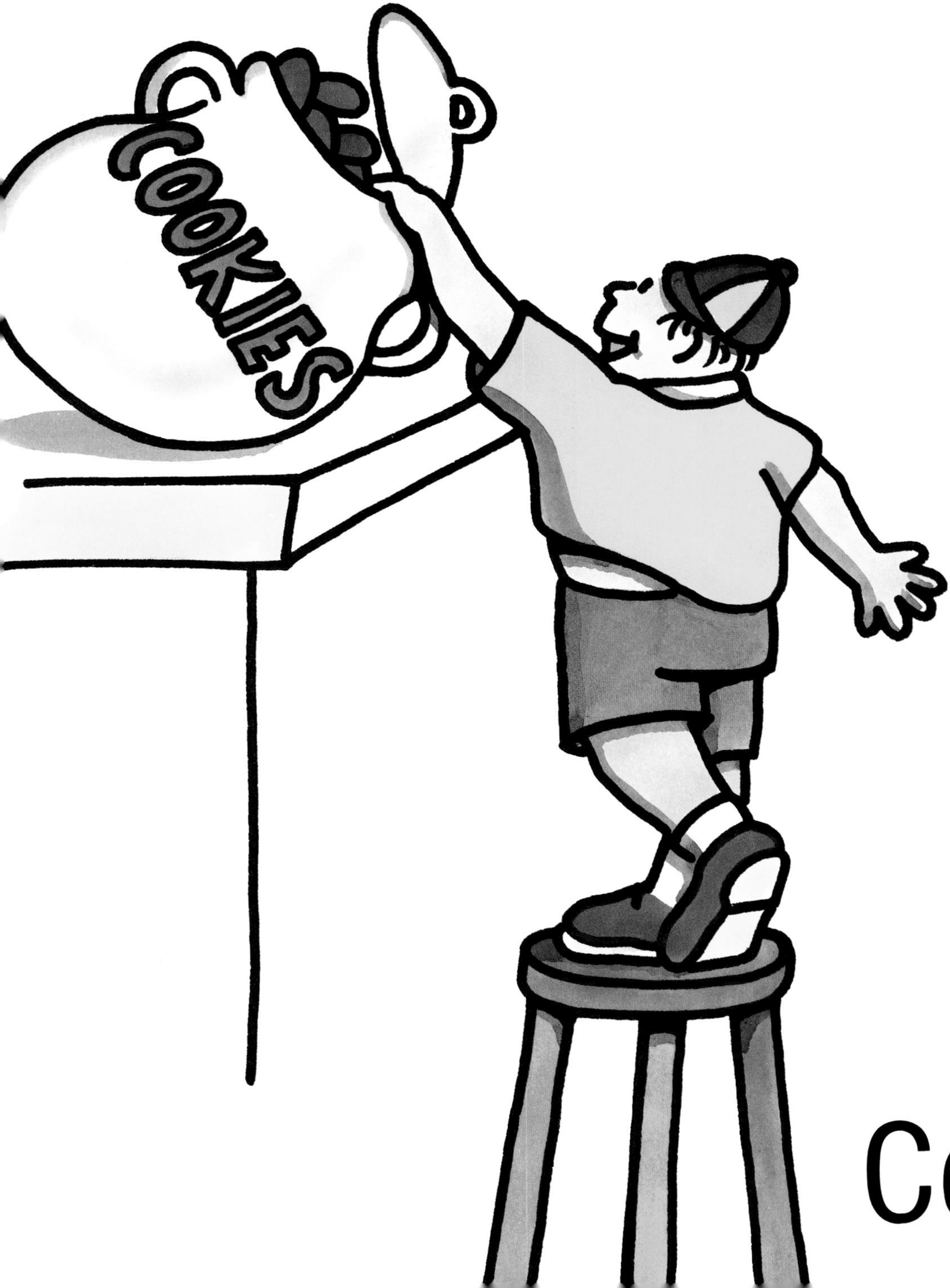

Cookies

Popcorn

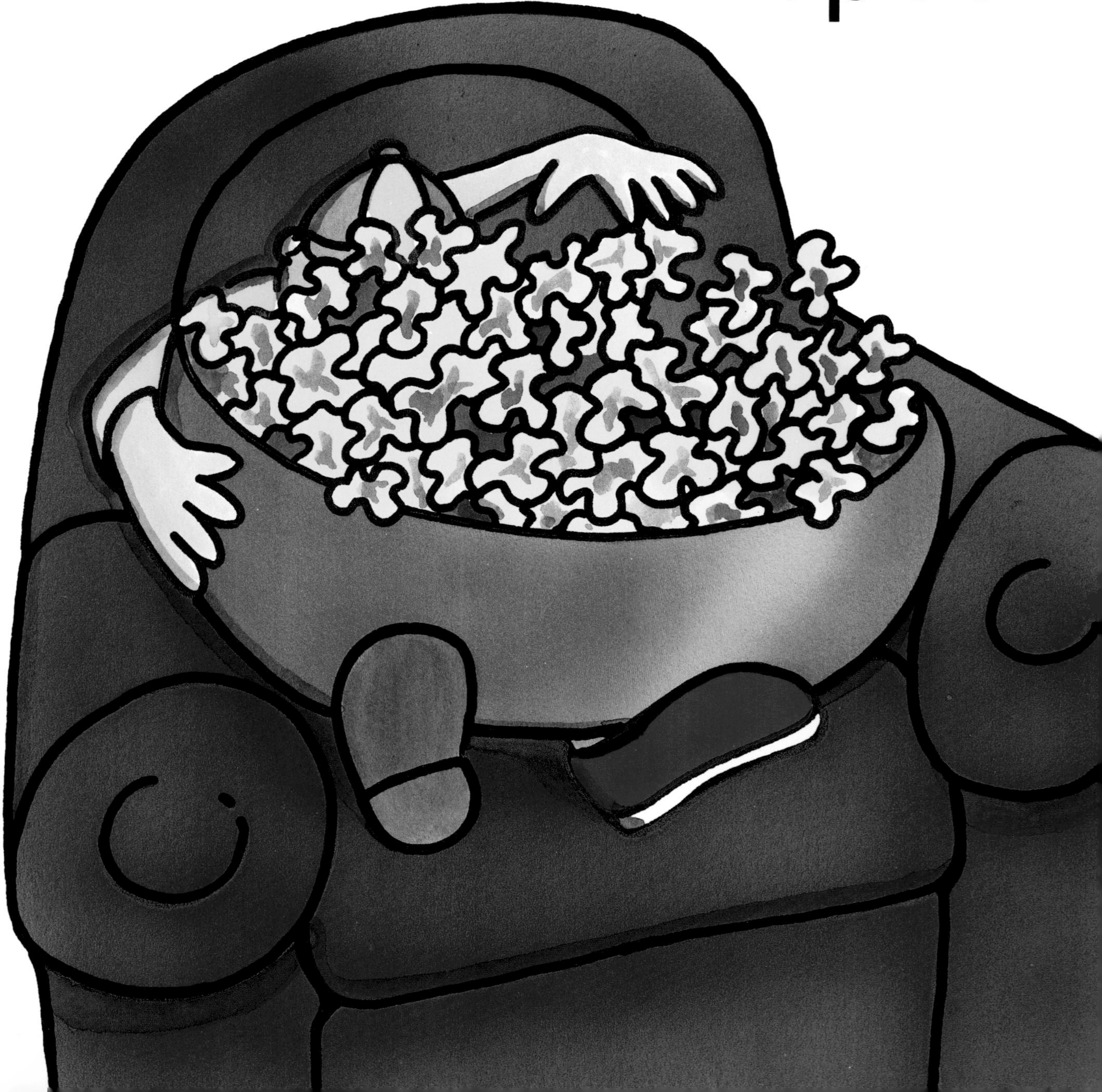

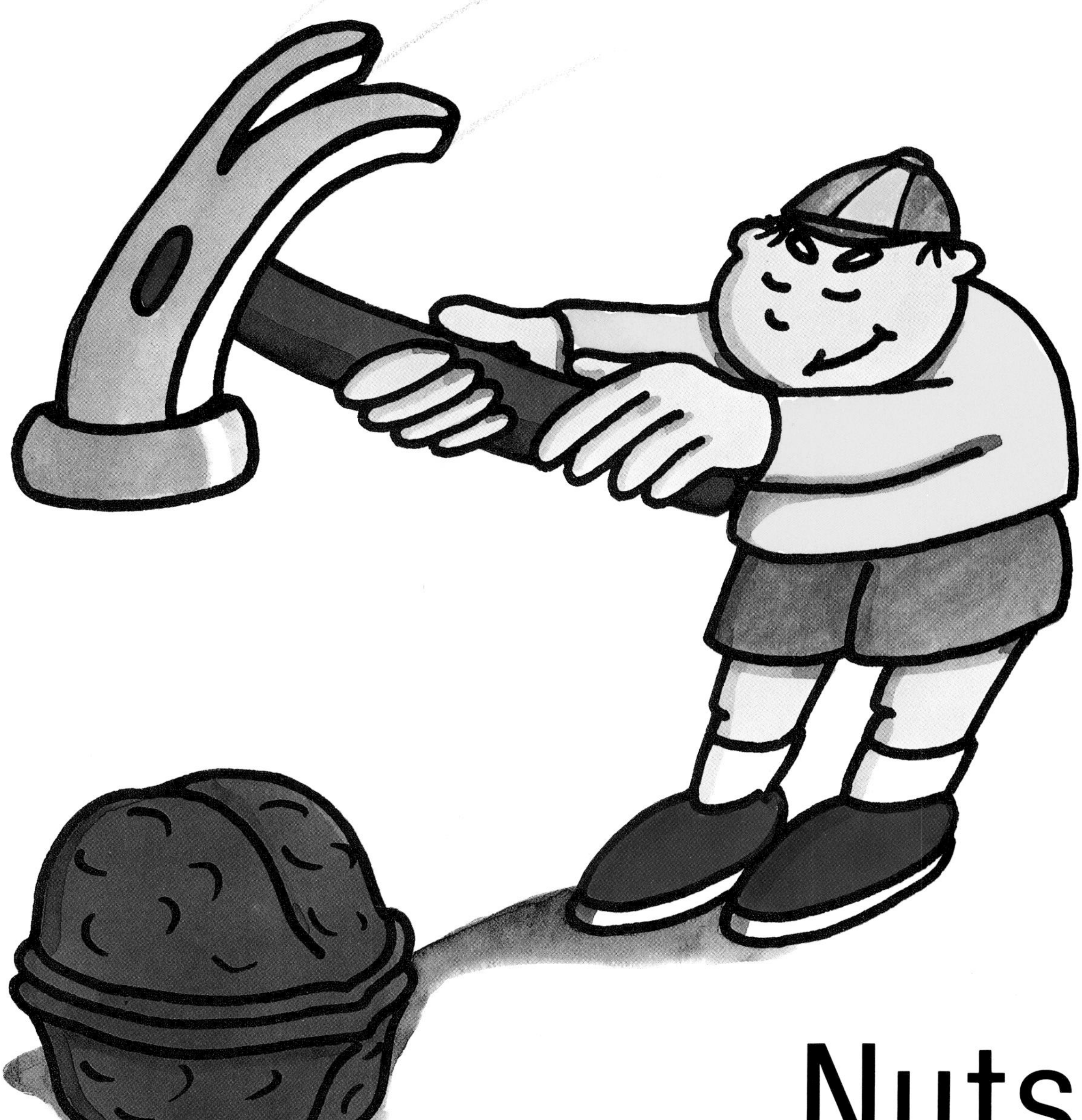

Nuts

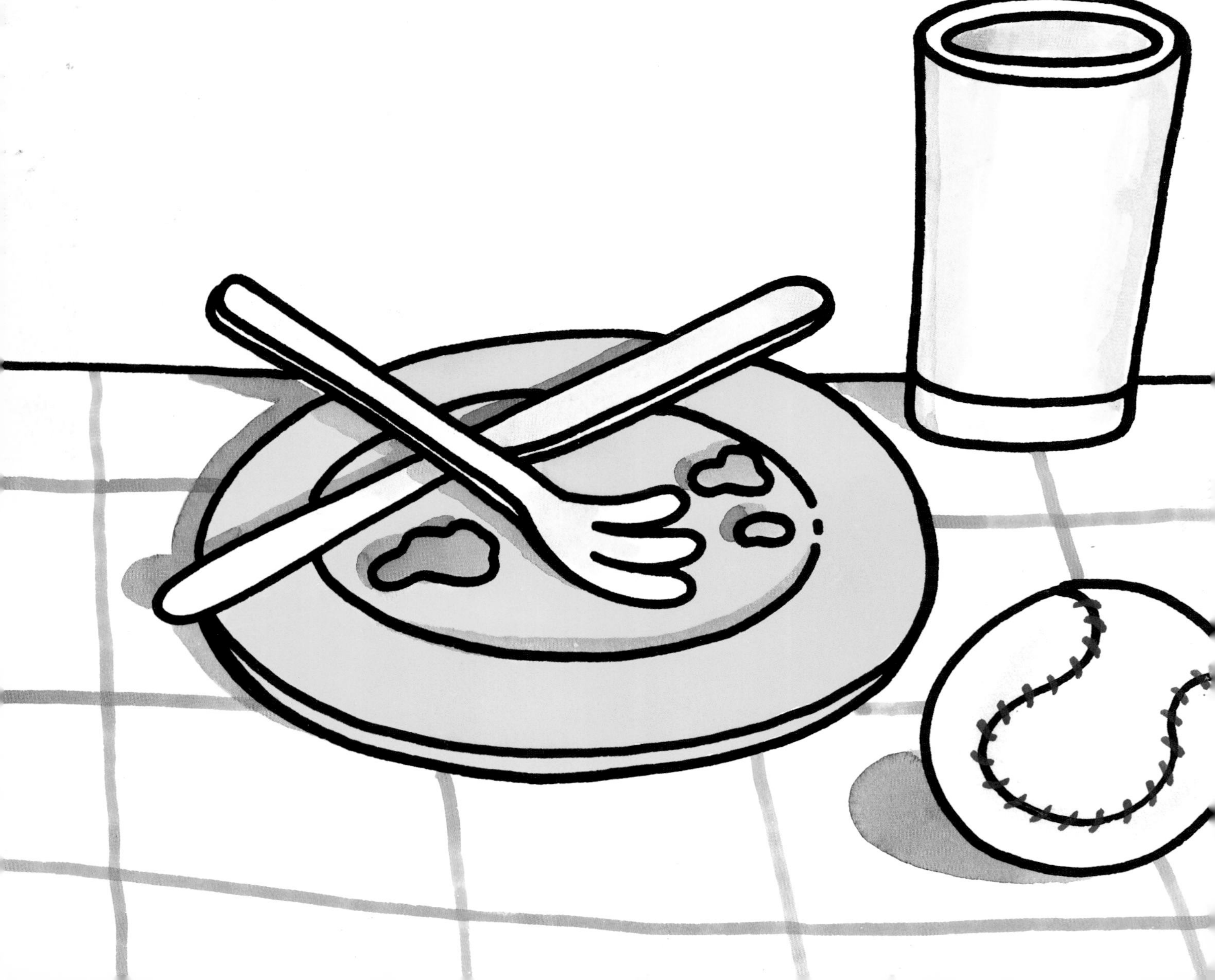